Profiles of the Presidents

JAMES EARL CARTER JR.

★ ★ ★

Profiles of the Presidents

JAMES EARL CARTER JR.

by Andrew Santella

Content Adviser: E. Stanly Godbold, Department of History, Mississippi State University

Reading Adviser: Dr. Linda D. Labbo, Department of Reading Education, College of Education, The University of Georgia

Compass Point Books
151 Good Counsel Drive
P.O. Box 669
Mankato, MN 56002-0669

Photographs ©: Hulton/Archive by Getty Images, cover, 3, 18, 27, 35, 37, 39, 41, 44 (all), 45, 56 (bottom right), 57 (right); Bettmann/Corbis, 6, 9, 11, 16, 19, 20, 21, 23, 28, 32, 42, 43, 54 (left), 56 (left), 57 (left); Owen Franken/Corbis, 8, 25, 26; Franz-Marc Frei/Corbis, 10; Corbis, 12, 13, 14; Jimmy Carter Library & Museum, 15, 17, 29, 30, 33, 34, 36, 55 (left); Hulton-Deutsch Collection/ Corbis, 31; Wally McNamee/Corbis, 38; Jerry Cooke/Corbis, 40; Dave G Houser/Corbis, 47, 59 (left); AFP/Corbis, 48; Reuters NewMedia Inc./Corbis, 49, 50; Stock Montage, 54 (right); Franklin D. Roosevelt Library, 55 (right); Galen Rowell/Corbis, 56 (top right); Bob Krist/Corbis, 58; PhotoDisc, 59 (top right); NASA, 59 (bottom right).

Editors: E. Russell Primm, Emily J. Dolbear, Melissa McDaniel, and Catherine Neitge
Photo Researcher: Svetlana Zhurkina
Photo Selector: Linda S. Koutris
Designer: The Design Lab
Cartographer: XNR Productions, Inc.

Library of Congress Cataloging-in-Publication Data
Santella, Andrew.
  James Earl Carter Jr. / by Andrew Santella.
    v. cm.— (Profiles of the presidents)
  Includes bibliographical references and index.
  Contents: "Jimmy Who?"—A boyhood in Plains—To Annapolis and beyond—Coming home—A run for the White House—A new kind of President—Setbacks for the President—Beyond the White House—Glossary—James Earl Carter's life at a glance—James Earl Carter's life and times—World events—Understanding James Earl Carter and his Presidency.
    ISBN 978-0-7565-0283-6
  1. Carter, Jimmy, 1924– —Juvenile literature. 2. Presidents—United States—Biography—Juvenile literature. [1. Carter, Jimmy, 1924– 2. Presidents.] I. Title. II. Series.
  E873 .S257 2003
  973.926'092—dc21   2002003031

Visit Compass Point Books on the Internet at *www.compasspointbooks.com*
or e-mail your request to *custserv@compasspointbooks.com*

Table of Contents

★ ★ ★

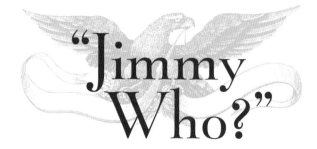

"Jimmy Who?"

★ ★ ★

The man from Georgia certainly seemed confident. For two years he traveled around America, walking up to people he had never met and saying, "Hi, I'm Jimmy Carter, and I'm going to be your next president."

The trouble was, very few of those people believed Jimmy Carter would ever be president of the United States. In fact, in early 1976, few people had even heard of

James Earl Carter Jr. ▶

him. Even after he introduced himself, many could only ask, "Jimmy who?" Carter had been governor of Georgia for four years. Before that, he had served two terms in the state senate. Some of the other people who were running for president had years and years of experience in politics. Compared to them, Jimmy Carter was just a beginner.

But Carter was determined to become the Democratic Party's **candidate** for president. He had made up his mind to win the 1976 presidential election. He may not have been as well-known as the other candidates, but nobody worked harder. Carter spent most of 1975 and 1976 on the campaign trail, meeting voters all across the United States. He gave speeches, attended rallies, and shook thousands of hands. Little by little, American voters got to know Jimmy Carter. His confidence impressed them, and so did his hard work.

Carter had something else going for him—good timing. In 1974, President Richard Nixon had **resigned** from his office in disgrace. He had to leave because he had tried to cover up his employees' crimes. Many American voters lost their faith in politicians and in government. By 1976, they were looking for a new kind of leader—someone more honest, someone they could trust. They wanted a leader who would bring change to the nation's capital and restore their faith in government.

In 1976, Carter convinced American voters that he was that leader. Before long, people weren't calling him "Jimmy who." They were calling him "Mr. President."

Jimmy Carter won the support and trust of American people.

A Boyhood in Plains

★ ★ ★

Plains, Georgia, is a small town surrounded by farms that produce cotton, peanuts, and other crops. There, on

October 1, 1924, Lillian Carter and James Earl Carter welcomed their first child into the world. They named their baby boy James Earl Carter Jr., after his father, but they would always call their son Jimmy.

By the time Jimmy was born, his father had become one of the most respected businessmen in

Jimmy Carter at age one

Jimmy Carter grew up in this house in Plains, Georgia.

Plains. He owned a successful peanut farm and served as a **deacon** in the Plains Baptist Church. The Carters were well off, but they led a simple life. The family house stood alongside a dirt road about 3 miles (4.8 kilometers) outside Plains. When Jimmy was very young, the house had neither electricity nor running water. And, instead of a lush lawn, the backyard was covered with white sand.

Jimmy was the oldest of four children. He had two sisters—Gloria and Ruth—and a brother—Billy. Jimmy's mother was a nurse, but she gave up her job when Jimmy was born. After that, she devoted herself to being a full-time wife and mother. She taught Jimmy to read when he was four years old. She also taught him important lessons about respecting people of all colors.

When Jimmy Carter was a boy, small towns like Plains were divided by race. African-Americans and whites went to different schools and worshiped in different churches. Sometimes it seemed like whites and African-Americans lived in two different worlds in one town.

Lillian Carter would have none of this. As a nurse, she had earned the trust of African-American women and their families in Plains. Unlike some of the white people in

▼ *Jimmy Carter and his family in 1953*

Like churches and ▸ schools in the town where Jimmy Carter grew up, this southern lunchroom was divided by race.

Plains, she welcomed African-Americans into her home. "When her black friends came to our home, she encouraged them to come through the front door," Jimmy Carter later remembered. "And she treated them like equals." She provided an example of respect and fairness that her son would long remember.

From his father, Jimmy learned much about the business of farming. His father was a strict but fair man who always demanded that Jimmy do his best. Even as a boy, Jimmy was expected to help out on the farm. He hauled drinking water to workers sweating in the hot Georgia sun. He trimmed vines and pulled weeds. He fed and cleaned up after the hogs and other farm animals. By the time he was

thirteen, Jimmy knew how to wash and boil the peanuts
the family grew. In his spare time, Jimmy hauled peanuts
into town in a wagon and sold them. His little business did
well, and Jimmy saved enough money to buy a few modest
houses in Plains. He rented them to farm families, and the
monthly rents added to his savings.

At school, Jimmy was a member of the debate team,
the book club, and the Future Farmers of America.
Throughout grade school and high school, he was one of

◄ Even at a young
age, Jimmy helped
take care of the
animals on the
family farm.

the best students in his class. He also played on his high school's basketball and baseball teams. When he graduated from high school in 1941, Jimmy was chosen to deliver a speech to his classmates and their families.

Even before he entered high school, Jimmy had made up his mind to go to college. He knew just which college he wanted to attend, too. He was determined to enroll in

Jimmy Carter (far left, back row) played for his high school's basketball team.

the United States Naval Academy in Annapolis, Maryland. Jimmy's uncle Tom Gordy served in the U.S. Navy. Jimmy loved to look at the postcards his uncle sent him from faraway places he visited.

Jimmy was so thrilled by Uncle Tom's adventures that he read every book he could find about the navy and the Naval Academy. He wrote to the Naval Academy to find out what high school classes he should take to be admitted there. He worried that his education in Plains would not prepare him for the navy. He even worried that the navy might reject him because his teeth did not line up properly!

He need not have worried, however. Jimmy was accepted to the Naval Academy in 1942. To prepare for his studies there, Jimmy went to nearby Southwestern College in 1941. The next year he studied science at the Georgia Institute of Technology in faraway Atlanta. Finally, in the summer of 1943 he left Georgia to start his new life in the U.S. Navy.

◄ *Carter (front row, far right) and fellow students at Southwestern College*

To Annapolis and Back

* * *

When Jimmy Carter arrived at the Naval Academy in 1943, the United States was fighting World War II (1939–1945). The navy needed so many new officers that it rushed its wartime trainees through their classes. Those in Jimmy Carter's class completed their studies in three years instead of the usual four. Carter packed a great deal of learning into those three years. He studied electronics, took flight training, and even practiced ballroom dancing and delivering speeches. He graduated near the top of his class.

On one of his trips home from the Naval Academy, Carter met a

A yearbook picture ▶ of Carter from his days at the Naval Academy

friend of his sister
Ruth. Her name was
Rosalynn Smith. She
had grown up in
Plains, but she was
three years younger
than Carter. The two
began dating and soon
fell in love. One
month after his gradu-
ation, they were mar-
ried in Plains.

After graduating,
Carter became a lieu-
tenant in the navy and he began an eight-year tour of
service. Carter chose to work on submarines, one of the
navy's most demanding duties. He had to spend weeks
at a time at sea.

▲ *Jimmy and Rosalynn Carter on their wedding day in 1946*

Of course, that meant that he and his new wife were
apart from each other much of the time. Soon Rosalynn
had to care for a growing family on her own. In 1947,
the Carters had their first child, a boy named John
William. They would have two more boys—James Earl

Jimmy Carter with his family in 1976

III was born in 1950, and Donnel Jeffrey was born in 1952. Their only daughter, Amy Lynn, arrived in 1967.

As an officer in the navy, Carter traveled all around the world. He worked on developing a new kind of submarine that ran on nuclear power. This project was headed by Captain Hyman Rickover, one of the navy's toughest commanders. As a member of Rickover's research team, Carter had to work harder than ever. Like Carter's father, Rickover always demanded that Carter do his best. Later, Carter would say that his father and Rickover were the two most important men in his life.

In 1953, Carter's father became ill with cancer. On July 23 of that year, he died. Besides dealing with his father's death, Carter now had to make an important decision. His family needed him in Plains. Someone had to run the family farm and business. It was now his mother's only source of income. If Jimmy didn't come home, the family might lose the farm. Of course, returning home would mean giving up his career in the navy.

Carter decided that family came first. He resigned from the navy and returned to Plains to take over the family farm.

◄ *Carter returned to work on the family peanut farm after his father's death in 1953.*

After eight years in the navy, the small town of Plains seemed very quiet to Carter. He found plenty to keep him busy, however. In his first year running the farm, there was little rain, and many of the crops died.

But Carter had decided to make the family farm thrive once more. He worked just as hard on the farm as he had in the navy. He took classes in business management and in agriculture. He introduced new farming methods and expanded the family's business. Rosalynn helped, as well. Within five years, the family business was more successful than ever. What's more, Carter began to follow in his father's footsteps as a leader in the town. He became a deacon and Sunday school teacher at Plains Baptist Church. He served as a member of the local school board.

Carter served as both a deacon and a Sunday school teacher at the Plains Baptist Church.

As a community leader, Carter took a stand against injustice in Plains. In 1958, a group of Plains residents formed a local chapter of a national group called the White Citizens Council. The council believed in segregation—the practice of separating blacks and whites by having different schools, waiting rooms, and even drinking fountains. Nearly every white man in Plains joined the new chapter of the White Citizens Council. But Jimmy Carter refused to join.

The White Citizens Council organized a **boycott** of Carter's warehouse. The group's members refused to buy his products, such as seeds and fertilizer. The boycott did

◄ Segregation meant that blacks and whites had to use separate doors to enter a building.

not destroy Carter's business, though. The warehouse just kept thriving.

Experiences like these made Carter believe that places such as Plains had to change. His work on the local school board had taught him that the best place to create change was in Atlanta, the state capital. So in 1962, Carter ran for a seat in the Georgia state senate. Carter lost the **primary** election. When he proved that the other man had cheated in the election, however, a judge declared that Carter had actually won the primary. Carter went on to win the seat in the Georgia state senate.

Carter served in the state senate for four years. During that time, he pushed for changes in Georgia's education system. He also fought against laws designed to keep African-Americans from voting. After his second two-year term in the senate, Carter set his sights on a higher goal. He decided to run for governor.

Carter was in for a surprise, however. Georgia voters were not ready for his strong stand against segregation. He finished a distant third in the voting for who would be the Democratic candidate.

Carter was stunned and hurt by the defeat. He quickly made up his mind to run for governor again in the 1970 election. He spent the next four years traveling all over Georgia, giving speeches and meeting with political leaders. His hard work paid off. He won the 1970 election for governor, and the Carter family moved into the governor's mansion in Atlanta.

Carter instantly made his mark as governor. In his first speech, he declared that "the time for racial

▾ *Jimmy Carter meeting with the state senate during his term as governor of Georgia*

discrimination is over." No other southern governor had ever said anything like that. The speech made headlines all over the country.

As governor, Carter made a point of hiring more African-Americans to fill jobs in state government. He also worked to protect Georgia's environment and to provide more money for schools.

At that time, Georgia law allowed governors to serve just one term. As a result, when Carter's term as governor ended in 1974, he had to find new political challenges.

Even before he left the governor's mansion, though, Carter had made up his mind about his future. One day in 1973, his mother asked him what he would do next. He said that he planned to run for president. His mother asked, "President of what?" Carter replied, "I'm going to run for president of the United States, and I'm going to win. "

A Run for the White House

★ ★ ★

One month before he left the Georgia governor's office, Jimmy Carter announced to the nation that he was running for president. The election of 1976 was still nearly two years away, but Carter was already preparing for his presidential campaign.

In 1972, he led a Democratic Party group that worked to elect Democrats to governor's offices across the country. In 1974, he became chairman of the Democratic National Campaign Committee. As chairman, he oversaw all the party's campaign activities. He also met most of the

▾ *Carter's presidential campaign headquarters in Plains, Georgia*

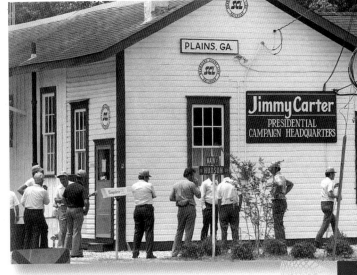

nation's top Democrats. Many of these people would help him in his run for president.

Carter kicked off his campaign by hitting the road and traveling all across the United States. He spent most of 1975 away from home, meeting voters and telling them what kind of president he would be. His campaign slogan was "A leader, for a change."

He hoped that American voters were ready for a change. The public's trust in government had been badly shaken by the scandal that had driven President Richard Nixon from office. Carter offered himself as a

Carter tells voters what kind of a president he would be.

new, more honest kind of leader. "I will never lie to you," he said again and again.

No matter what he did and how hard he worked, though, Carter had a hard time attracting much attention. He was one of nine Democrats campaigning to be the party's presidential candidate, and some of the others were much better known than Carter.

So it was a huge surprise for most people when Carter won early primary contests in Iowa and New Hampshire. Suddenly, everyone wanted to know who Jimmy Carter was! He kept on winning primary elections, until most of the other Democrats dropped out of the race. Amazingly, "Jimmy who" became the

Democratic candidate for president. He chose Senator Walter Mondale of Minnesota as his vice presidential running mate.

Carter faced President Gerald R. Ford in the election. Ford had been Nixon's vice president and after Nixon resigned in 1974, Ford became president. He had much more experience in national government than Carter did. But Carter did very well in television debates with Ford.

Jimmy Carter and Gerald Ford in a televised debate ▶

The election of 1976 was close, but Carter won. He captured 297 electoral votes to Ford's 240. On January 20, 1977, Carter was sworn in as the thirty-ninth president of the United States.

▼ *Carter is sworn in as president.*

A New Kind of President

★ ★ ★

Jimmy Carter had promised to be a new kind of president. On his first day in office, he showed the nation what he meant. When he was sworn in, he wore an ordinary business suit, rather than a top hat and tuxedo as other presidents had. Instead of riding in a limousine during the parade, he walked. From the start, Carter

Carter shows that ▶ he is a new and informal president during this casual discussion with reporters.

tried to show that the president of the United States could live and work like an ordinary American.

Carter wanted the people who worked with him to represent all Americans. He appointed African-Americans and women to important positions. Patricia Roberts Harris, an African-American, was named secretary of housing and urban development. Juanita M. Kreps became secretary of commerce. Carter also appointed African-American congressman Andrew Young as **ambassador** to the United Nations.

◀ United Nations ambassador Andrew Young, right, meets with British foreign secretary Anthony Crossland.

Like most new presidents, Carter quickly set a number of new policies. His first major decision was to give **pardons** to people who had evaded the draft during the Vietnam War. That war had caused deep conflict in the United States. Many Americans had not approved of U.S. involvement in this war. Some people left the country to avoid having to fight in the war. Carter's pardon allowed these people to return to the United States without fear of punishment. Many people were against the pardons. Carter, however, believed that the pardons would help Americans put their disagreements over the Vietnam War behind them.

In May 1975, New York congresswoman Bella Abzug called for a presidential pardon for Vietnam draft resisters. President Carter did just that after becoming president.

In his first year as president, Carter worked successfully with Congress on a number of issues. He convinced Congress to lower taxes and to create a new Department of Energy.

Early in his presidency, Carter also announced that the United States would place a new importance on **human rights** around the world. Carter was concerned that many countries were denying people their basic rights. For example, some governments abused prisoners or kept people from worshiping as they wished. Carter decided that the United States would no longer send money or products to such countries.

◀ *Jimmy Carter speaks with his secretary of energy, James Schlesinger.*

In 1977, Carter made another important decision. He said that he wanted to give control of the Panama Canal to the country of Panama. The Panama Canal is a waterway that cuts across that narrow Central American country. It was built between 1904 and 1914 to connect the Atlantic and Pacific Oceans. From the time it was built, the canal had been under U.S. control. Carter believed that because the canal was in Panama, it should be controlled by Panama. Carter worked out a **treaty** with Panama. Then he had to send it to the U.S. Senate for approval. Some senators were determined to stop the treaty. In time, though, the Senate agreed to the treaty.

Jimmy Carter and ▶ Panamanian leader Omar Torrijos at the signing of their famous treaty, which turned over control of the Panama Canal to Panama

Carter also worked to improve the relationship between the United States and China. Relations between the two countries had been strained ever since a **communist** government had taken control of China in 1949. In 1979, the United States and China exchanged ambassadors for the first time.

Perhaps Carter's greatest achievement was arranging a peace treaty between Egypt and Israel. The two nations had been fighting over territory for years.

◄ *Jimmy Carter worked with Chinese leader Den Xiaoping to improve relations between their countries.*

In 1978, Carter invited President Anwar el-Sadat of Egypt and Prime Minister Menachem Begin of Israel to attend peace talks. Sadat, Carter, and Begin met at Camp David, the presidential retreat in Maryland. After thirteen days of tense discussions in September, Egypt and Israel agreed to a peace treaty. Sadat and Begin returned to Washington and signed the treaty on March 26, 1979, with a beaming President Carter looking on.

Jimmy Carter ▾ arranged a meeting at Camp David between Menachem Begin (left) and Anwar el-Sadat.

Setbacks for the President

★   ★   ★

As his term went on, however, Carter had fewer successes. From the first days of his presidency, Carter was determined to reduce the amount of oil the United States needed to buy from other countries. He wanted Americans to conserve energy by driving their cars less often and by using less heating fuel. He also wanted the government to develop new sources of energy, such as wind power and solar energy.

◂ *Solar homes rely on the sun as a source of energy.*

Gasoline shortages made Carter unpopular with people like these protesters.

But Carter had a hard time convincing Congress to make his energy plan a law. By 1978, gasoline shortages raised the prices that Americans had to pay for gas. Many blamed Carter for those high prices.

Carter succeeded in reducing the amount of foreign oil Americans used, though. His policies also helped build greater supplies of energy for the future, but he received little credit for these achievements.

By 1979, many Americans were questioning Carter's leadership. Oil and food prices were high. An increasing number of Americans were out of work.

In an effort to regain the people's trust, Carter decided to make changes in his advisers. He replaced six **cabinet** members with new people.

Still, the setbacks kept coming. At that time, the United States and the Soviet Union were the two most powerful nations in the world. In 1979, Carter worked out a treaty with the Soviet Union that would limit the use of nuclear weapons. But the U.S. Senate never got the chance to vote on the treaty. Late in 1979, the

▾ *Jimmy Carter and Soviet leader Leonid Brezhnev*

Opening ceremony of the 1980 Olympics

Soviet Union invaded Afghanistan. To protest this, Carter asked the Senate not to vote on the treaty. He also organized a boycott of the 1980 Olympic Games, which were held in the Soviet capital of Moscow. He also asked Congress for money to build up the U.S. military.

On November 4, 1979, Carter received the worst news of his presidency. Thousands of protesters in Teheran, the capital of Iran, had taken over the United States **embassy**. They held fifty-two American citizens hostage for more than a year.

The Iranian government demanded that the United States return the former shah, or leader, of Iran to that country. Iran wanted the shah to stand trial for crimes against the people of Iran. The shah had ruled Iran from

▲ *One of fifty-two Americans taken hostage by Iran in 1979*

1941 to 1979, when he was overthrown in a revolution.
He later moved to the United States for medical treatment.

Carter refused to return the shah to Iran. Instead,
he cut off all relations with Iran and refused to let
Iranian oil or goods be sold in the United States.

He also approved plans for a mission to rescue the
hostages. The rescue mission was a disaster, however. In

April 1980, an American military plane and a helicopter collided on their way to attempt a rescue. Eight crew members were killed.

▲ A U.S. helicopter lies destroyed after a failed rescue mission in Iran.

The hostages remained in captivity month after month. The longer they were held, the more people seemed to blame Carter.

The hostage crisis also drew attention away from Carter's success in establishing the Department of Education in 1980. People gave little thought to the work he had done to help women, African-Americans, and students.

As the 1980 election approached, Senator Edward Kennedy of Massachusetts—a Democrat—announced that he was running for president. Presidents rarely face

a serious challenge from within their own party. Kennedy's decision meant that Carter would have to spend energy and money to defeat Kennedy in primary elections.

Senator Edward Kennedy (right) ran against Carter in the 1980 primary elections.

Congressman John Anderson ran as an independent in the general election.

Carter succeeded in defeating Kennedy and becoming the Democratic candidate. The effort left his campaign weakened and the party divided.

In the general election, Carter faced an even tougher challenge from Republican Ronald Reagan, the former

governor of California. Then, another candidate—
Congressman John Anderson of Illinois—entered the
race as an independent.

This time, the challenge proved to be too much.
Reagan won the presidency easily, capturing 489
electoral votes to just 49 for Carter.

▾ *Ronald and Nancy Reagan*

Beyond the White House

★ ★ ★

During his last weeks in office, Carter continued to work to free the hostages. They were finally released on January 20, 1981—Ronald Reagan's first day as president. Losing the election and failing to free the hostages while he was still president saddened Carter. Still, he

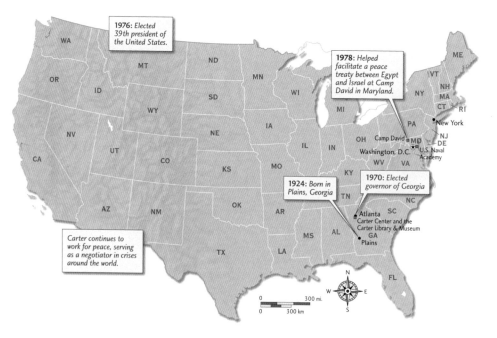

1976: *Elected 39th president of the United States.*

1978: *Helped facilitate a peace treaty between Egypt and Israel at Camp David in Maryland.*

1924: *Born in Plains, Georgia*

1970: *Elected governor of Georgia*

Carter continues to work for peace, serving as a negotiator in crises around the world.

Camp David
Washington, D.C.
U.S. Naval Academy
New York
Atlanta
Carter Center and the Carter Library & Museum
Plains

0   300 mi.
0   300 km

continued to look forward to new challenges. He was only fifty-six years old when left the White House. As he later put it, "I was not ready for retirement."

Instead of retiring, Carter became one of the most active former presidents in history. On October 1, 1986, he formally opened the Carter Presidential Center of Emory University in Atlanta to promote democracy, human rights, and health care throughout the world.

▾ *The Carter Presidential Center is located at Emory University in Atlanta, Georgia.*

He has continued to travel the world to promote democracy. To make sure voting is conducted honestly, he has supervised elections in countries such as the Dominican Republic and Nicaragua. In May 2002, Carter became the first U.S. president to visit Cuba since Fidel Castro took over its government. He took this opportunity to meet with Cubans, and to speak to the people directly through a television address. He encouraged Castro to make democratic reforms.

In May 2002, Jimmy ▶ Carter made history by traveling to Cuba to meet with its leader, Fidel Castro.

Carter also continues to work hard closer to home. He volunteers as a carpenter with Habitat for Humanity, a group that builds new homes for poor people. He has served as a deacon and Sunday school teacher at his local church. He has also published many books, including a book of poetry.

▾ *Jimmy and Rosalynn Carter build homes for Habitat for Humanity.*

Carter has received much praise for his active life after leaving the presidency, but he achieved a great deal while he was president, too. His role in helping Israel and Egypt reach a peace agreement stands as an example for every president who follows him. So did his tireless work to promote human rights around the world. In 1999, Jimmy and Rosalynn Carter each received the

Both Jimmy and Rosalynn Carter have been awarded the Presidential Medal of Freedom.

Presidential Medal of Freedom, the highest award an American citizen can be given. It was a fitting honor for a president who returned high ideals—and a common touch—to the White House.

GLOSSARY

★ ★ ★

ambassador—the representative of a nation's government in another country

boycott—a refusal to do business with someone as a form of protest

cabinet—a president's group of advisers

candidate—someone running for office in an election

communist—an economic system in which all businesses are owned by the government

deacon—someone who helps a minister in a Christian church

discrimination—treating people unfairly because of their race, religion, sex, or age

embassy—a building in one country where the representatives of another country work

human rights—the basic rights that every person in the world should have

pardons—acts that forgive crimes, so that the people who committed the crimes are not punished

primary—an election that decides who will be a party's candidate in the general election

resigned—gave up a job or position

treaty—an agreement between two governments

JAMES EARL CARTER JR.'S LIFE AT A GLANCE

★ ★ ★

PERSONAL

Nickname:	Jimmy
Born:	October 1, 1924
Birthplace:	Plains, Georgia
Father's name:	James Earl Carter
Mother's name:	Lillian Gordy Carter
Education:	Graduated from the U.S. Naval Academy in Annapolis, Maryland, in 1946
Wife's name:	Rosalynn Smith Carter
Married:	July 7, 1946
Children:	John William "Jack" Carter (1947–); James Earl "Chip" Carter III (1950–); Donnel Jeffrey "Jeff" Carter (1952–); Amy Lynn Carter (1967–)

PUBLIC

Occupation before presidency: Farmer, public official

Occupation after presidency: Statesman

Military service: Navy

Other government positions: Georgia state senator, governor of Georgia

Political party: Democrat

Vice president: Walter F. Mondale (1977–1981)

Dates in office: January 20, 1977–January 20, 1981

Presidential opponents: President Gerald R. Ford (Republican), 1976; Ronald Reagan (Republican) and John Anderson (independent), 1980

Number of votes (Electoral College): 40,827,394 of 79,973,371, (297 of 538), 1976; 34,964,583 of 83,820,686, (49 of 538), 1980

Selected Writings: *Why Not the Best?* (1975), *A Government as Good as Its People* (1977), *Keeping Faith* (1982), *Negotiation* (1984), *The Blood of Abraham* (1985), *Turning Point* (1992), *Talking Peace* (1993), *Living Faith* (1996), *Sources of Strength* (1997), *The Virtues of Aging* (1997), *As Time Goes By* (2001), *Christmas in Plains* (2001)

★

James Earl Carter Jr.'s Cabinet

Secretary of state:
  Cyrus R. Vance (1977–1980)
  Edmund S. Muskie (1980–1981)

Secretary of the treasury:
  W. Michael Blumenthal (1977–1979)
  G. William Miller (1979–1981)

Secretary of defense:
  Harold Brown (1977–1981)

Attorney general:
  Griffin B. Bell (1977–1979)
  Benjamin R. Civiletti (1979–1981)

Secretary of the interior:
  Cecil D. Andrus (1977–1981)

Secretary of agriculture:
  Robert S. Bergland (1977–1981)

Secretary of commerce:
  Juanita M. Kreps (1977–1979)
  Philip Klutznick (1979–1981)

Secretary of labor:
  F. Ray Marshall (1977–1981)

Secretary of health, education, and welfare:
  Joseph A. Califano Jr. (1977–1979)
  Patricia R. Harris (1979–1980)

Secretary of health and human services:
  Patricia R. Harris (1980–1981)

Secretary of education:
  Shirley Hufstedler (1980–1981)

Secretary of housing and urban development:
  Patricia R. Harris (1977–1979)
  Moon Landrieu (1979–1981)

Secretary of transportation:
  Brock Adams (1977–1979)
  Neil E. Goldschmidt (1979–1981)

Secretary of energy:
  James R. Schlesinger (1977–1979)
  Charles W. Duncan Jr. (1979–1981)

JAMES EARL CARTER JR.'S LIFE AND TIMES

★ ★ ★

CARTER'S LIFE

October 1, James Earl Carter Jr. (below) is born — 1924

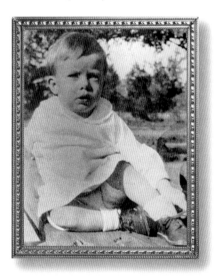

WORLD EVENTS

1926 — A.A. Milne publishes *Winnie the Pooh*

1928 — Penicillin, the first antibiotic, is discovered by Scottish scientist Alexander Fleming

1929 — The United States stock exchange collapses, and severe economic depression sets in

1930

1933 — Nazi leader Adolf Hitler (below) is named chancellor of Germany

CARTER'S LIFE

WORLD EVENTS

1939 German troops
invade Poland. Britain
and France declare
war on Germany.
World War II
(1939–45) begins.

Commercial tele-
vision is introduced
to America

1940

Graduates form Plains **1941**
High School

1941 December
7, Japanese
bombers
attack Pearl
Harbor,
Hawaii (right), and
America enters World
War II

1942 Japanese Americans
are placed in intern-
ment camps due to
fear of disloyalty

Graduates from the **1946**
United States Naval
Academy

July 7, marries
Rosalynn Smith
(above)

1945 America drops atomic
bombs on the Japanese
cities of Hiroshima
and Nagasaki to end
World War II

CARTER'S LIFE

WORLD EVENTS

1950

1949   Birth of the People's Republic of China

1953

Resigns from U.S. Navy to return home and run the family farm (below) after his father's death

1953   The first Europeans climb Mount Everest (below)

1959   Fidel Castro becomes prime minister of Cuba

Barbie doll debuts

1960

1961   Soviet cosmonaut Yuri Gagarin (below) is the first human to enter space

CARTER'S LIFE

Wins election to the   1962
Georgia Senate

Becomes governor of   1971
Georgia (above)

WORLD EVENTS

1962   U.S. author John
Steinbeck wins Nobel
Prize for literature

1963   Kenya becomes
an independent
republic (its first
president, Jomo
Kenyatta, is
pictured)

1964   G.I. Joe makes his
debut as the first boy's
"action figure"

1968   Civil rights leader
Martin Luther King
Jr. (above) is shot and
killed

1970

CARTER'S LIFE

WORLD EVENTS

1971   The first microprocessor is produced by Intel

Becomes the chairman of the Democratic Party's national campaign committee   1973

1973   Arab oil embargo creates concerns about natural resources

Spanish artist Pablo Picasso dies

Presidential Election Results:		Popular Votes	Electoral Votes
1976	James E. Carter Jr.	40,827,394	297
	Gerald R. Ford	39,145,977	240
1980	Ronald Reagan	43,276,489	489
	James E. Carter Jr.	34,964,583	49
	John Anderson	5,588,014	—

1974   Scientists find that chlorofluorocarbons—chemicals in coolants and propellants—are damaging Earth's ozone layer

1976   U.S. military academies admit women

The Department of Energy is founded   1977

Pardons Vietnam War draft evaders

The United States and Panama sign a treaty agreeing to return the Panama Canal to Panama on December 31, 1999

Helps arrange a peace treaty between Egypt and Israel   1978

1978   The first test-tube baby conceived outside its mother's womb is born in Oldham, England

The United States and China exchange ambassadors for the first time   1979

1979   The Soviet Union invades Afghanistan

November 4, protesters storm the U.S. Embassy in Iran and hold fifty-two Americans hostage

CARTER'S LIFE

The United States boycotts the Olympic Games in Moscow, the Soviet capital, in protest of the Soviet invasion of Afghanistan — 1980

January 20, the American hostages in Iran are freed — 1981

Becomes a distinguished professor at Emory University; opens the Carter Center (below) at Emory University, which works for human rights around the world — 1982

Receives the Presidential Medal of Freedom — 1999

Becomes the first U.S. president to visit Cuba under Fidel Castro's rule; awarded the Nobel Peace Prize — 2002

Offers his views on the Middle East in his controversial book "Palestine: Peace Not Apartheid" — 2006

WORLD EVENTS

1982 — Maya Lin designs the Vietnam Veterans Memorial (above), commemorating the Americans who died

1983 — The AIDS (acquired immune deficiency syndrome) virus is identified

1986 — The U.S. space shuttle *Challenger* explodes, killing all seven astronauts on board

2001 — Terrorist attacks on the two World Trade Center towers in New York City and on the Pentagon in Washington, D.C., leave thousands dead

2008 — May 12, a 7.9-magnitude earthquake strikes southwestern China, killing more than 62,000 people

1980

1990

2000

UNDERSTANDING JAMES EARL CARTER JR. AND HIS PRESIDENCY

★ ★ ★

FURTHER READING

George, Linda, and Charles George. *Jimmy Carter: Builder of Peace.* New York.: Children's Press, 2000.

Hobkirk, Lori. *James Earl Carter: Our Thirty-Ninth President.* Chanhassen, Minn.: The Child's World, 2002.

Joseph, Paul. *Jimmy Carter.* Minneapolis: Abdo & Daughters, 1999.

Schraff, Anne E. *Jimmy Carter.* Springfield, N.J.: Enslow Publishers, 1998.

Wade, Linda R. *James Carter.* Chicago: Childrens Press, 1989.

ON THE WEB

For more information on this topic, use FactHound.

1. Go to *www.facthound.com*
2. Type in this book ID: 0756502837
3. Click on the *Fetch It* button.

FactHound will find the best Web sites for you.

CARTER HISTORIC SITES
ACROSS THE COUNTRY

**Jimmy Carter National
Historic Site**
300 North Bond Street
Plains, GA 31780
229/824-4104
To visit President Carter's
boyhood farm and school

**Jimmy Carter Library and
Museum**
441 Freedom Parkway
Atlanta, GA 30307-1498
404/730-2215
To visit the former president's
library and museum

Georgia Governor's Mansion
391 West Paces Ferry Road, NW
Atlanta, GA 30308
404/261-1776
To tour the mansion where
President and Mrs. Carter lived
from 1971–1975, during his term
as governor of Georgia

JAMES EARL CARTER JR.

THE U.S. PRESIDENTS
(Years in Office)

★   ★   ★

1. **George Washington**
   (March 4, 1789–March 3, 1797)
2. **John Adams**
   (March 4, 1797–March 3, 1801)
3. **Thomas Jefferson**
   (March 4, 1801–March 3, 1809)
4. **James Madison**
   (March 4, 1809–March 3, 1817)
5. **James Monroe**
   (March 4, 1817–March 3, 1825)
6. **John Quincy Adams**
   (March 4, 1825–March 3, 1829)
7. **Andrew Jackson**
   (March 4, 1829–March 3, 1837)
8. **Martin Van Buren**
   (March 4, 1837–March 3, 1841)
9. **William Henry Harrison**
   (March 6, 1841–April 4, 1841)
10. **John Tyler**
    (April 6, 1841–March 3, 1845)
11. **James K. Polk**
    (March 4, 1845–March 3, 1849)
12. **Zachary Taylor**
    (March 5, 1849–July 9, 1850)
13. **Millard Fillmore**
    (July 10, 1850–March 3, 1853)
14. **Franklin Pierce**
    (March 4, 1853–March 3, 1857)
15. **James Buchanan**
    (March 4, 1857–March 3, 1861)
16. **Abraham Lincoln**
    (March 4, 1861–April 15, 1865)
17. **Andrew Johnson**
    (April 15, 1865–March 3, 1869)
18. **Ulysses S. Grant**
    (March 4, 1869–March 3, 1877)
19. **Rutherford B. Hayes**
    (March 4, 1877–March 3, 1881)
20. **James Garfield**
    (March 4, 1881–Sept 19, 1881)
21. **Chester Arthur**
    (Sept 20, 1881–March 3, 1885)
22. **Grover Cleveland**
    (March 4, 1885–March 3, 1889)
23. **Benjamin Harrison**
    (March 4, 1889–March 3, 1893)
24. **Grover Cleveland**
    (March 4, 1893–March 3, 1897)
25. **William McKinley**
    (March 4, 1897–September 14, 1901)
26. **Theodore Roosevelt**
    (September 14, 1901–March 3, 1909)
27. **William Howard Taft**
    (March 4, 1909–March 3, 1913)
28. **Woodrow Wilson**
    (March 4, 1913–March 3, 1921)
29. **Warren G. Harding**
    (March 4, 1921–August 2, 1923)
30. **Calvin Coolidge**
    (August 3, 1923–March 3, 1929)
31. **Herbert Hoover**
    (March 4, 1929–March 3, 1933)
32. **Franklin D. Roosevelt**
    (March 4, 1933–April 12, 1945)
33. **Harry S. Truman**
    (April 12, 1945–January 20, 1953)
34. **Dwight D. Eisenhower**
    (January 20, 1953–January 20, 1961)
35. **John F. Kennedy**
    (January 20, 1961–November 22, 1963)
36. **Lyndon B. Johnson**
    (November 22, 1963–January 20, 1969)
37. **Richard M. Nixon**
    (January 20, 1969–August 9, 1974)
38. **Gerald R. Ford**
    (August 9, 1974–January 20, 1977)
39. **James Earl Carter**
    (January 20, 1977–January 20, 1981)
40. **Ronald Reagan**
    (January 20, 1981–January 20, 1989)
41. **George H. W. Bush**
    (January 20, 1989–January 20, 1993)
42. **William Jefferson Clinton**
    (January 20, 1993–January 20, 2001)
43. **George W. Bush**
    (January 20, 2001–)

INDEX

★ ★ ★

ABOUT THE AUTHOR

Andrew Santella is a writer living in Cary, Illinois. He contributes to a wide range of publications, including *Gentlemen's Quarterly,* the *New York Times Magazine,* and *Commonweal.* He has written several books for children on the history of America.